Mr. Grievely
A Story of Grief and Love

Written by
Holly Margeson Gamache, M.Ed.

Illustrated by
Steve Hrehovcik

Mr. Grievely
A Story of Grief and Love

Written by Holly Margeson Gamache, M.Ed.

Illustrated by Steve Hrehovcik

Printed in the United States of America
Hollyhock Innovations, LLC

ISBN: 9798858896227

Graphic Design by Geraldine Aikman

Hollyhock Innovations, LLC
www.hollyhockinnovations.com
email library@hollyhockinnovations.com

Introduction

Grieving is a complex process with no clear road map. It can be fraught with judgment and expectation, either by those who are grieving or those who love them. Mr. Grievely offers a new perspective for anyone seeking guidance and relatability in their journey through grief.

There is a shortage of resources for grieving across the lifespan. Mr. Grievely masterfully fills that gap with humor, empathy and connection – meeting the needs of everyone from ten to one hundred and ten. It highlights the common thread in a process with vast variability.

Clinicians and non-clinicians alike should have a copy of Mr. Grievely on their shelf and should refer to it often.

~ Rebecca Mallen, LICSW

Dedication

"Mr. Grievely" is a dedication to the two most loving parents I could have ever been blessed to call Momma and Daddio, as well as the most wonderful mother-in-law, "Memere," I could have had. You continue to give, even beyond life, to me and to all your children and grandchildren. I can only hope you are all watching or standing by, helping those in the darkness to find a way through with the help of "Mr. Grievely." I owe so much to you and know we are never far apart. We see the hawks, eagles and cardinals, and find the feathers. We never question that you are just a breath away.

In memory and honor of

Charles (Chuck) E.D. Margeson, Jr.
Jo Anne (Jo) R. Margeson
Madelyn D. Gamache
Richard ("Unk") A. Maloney

Bubbles, Lola and Harvey,
always in our hearts.

Testimonials

As a lifelong funeral director, I have seen many clinicians and professionals explain what grief is. Having had a chance to read Mr. Grievely, I find it refreshing, and I think healthy, to see grief put into words and picture form for all to see, read and easily understand. Grief isn't something you get through. In its most healthy form, you learn to live with grief and eventually accept and live a full active life without it being dominated by grief.

~ Doug Bibber, Bibber Memorial Chapel

As a clinician, I have provided individual and group counseling to those who are experiencing grief. In Mr. Grievely, Holly Margeson Gamache eloquently gives voice to the challenges and vulnerability of grief work. Expect that Mr Grievely will be a source of comfort to both adults and children as they engage in the process of grieving.

~ Robert Vieira, LICSW

Forward

by Nancy Neri

Holly and I first met in 2016 and very quickly hit it off. Some people you are just drawn to, they feel like close friends from the first day, thus is our friendship.

When she asked me to write this forward I immediately said yes, but then thought, how am I going to do this? I know nothing about the art of writing. I soon recognized that I could write about what I did know.

I grew up surrounded by a world of loss and grief but for most of my life never felt it. You see, I am a funeral director, as was my father and his father before him. In my profession, when a death occurs we are called to care for the body of the deceased and at the same time – with skill, kindness and compassion – to guide their loved ones through the initial days of shock and disorientation until whatever services are chosen have concluded.

Holly tells the story of what happens next. The services are over and the real work of grieving begins – and believe me, it is work. Through "Mr. Grievely," Holly puts a face and identity to grief.

I faced my own grief with the loss of my dear parents. I have to say, working my way through it was it was one of the most difficult experiences of my life.

Through Holly's personal day-to-day struggle with grief, after the loss of her beloved mother and father, she created this moving and intimate story. "Mr. Grievely" follows the stages and emotions from denial and fear, step by step, all the way to eventual reconciliation with our loss. At first, we are afraid of Mr. Grievely, but along the way he becomes helpful, familiar, and eventually even a friend.

We, the readers, can feel that with each visit there is movement forward. Movement away from the sadness and bewilderment of living without the person we have loved. We see a way toward eventual acceptance of our loss and the path to embrace our new life.

Sorrow

Oh woe, and hello!
Mr. Grievely, come in.

You're lurking and peering,
much to my chagrin.

Standing off in grey shadows;
jumping up from behind.

You startle me so,
I'm certain to near lose my mind.

Where did you come from?
Did I invite you here?
You don't stand on ceremony,
that much is clear.

I was bobbing afloat
on this river of tears,
and it appears it was you
who capsized me, I fear.

In a moment's momentum,
without warning or clue,
plunged into a spiral,
tumbling downward askew.

Now engulfed in emotional
gushes and waves
that fill up my heart,
and my room and my days.

There are times in this whirlpool,
when I think I may drown,
but you pull out the plug,
and my sadness goes down.

These wet salty tears,
it's a taste I know well,
they're making my lips,
eyes and soul start to swell.

So exhausted and drained,
feeling weak from the weeping.
I am forced to lie down,
and to just keep on sleeping.

A smoky spell hovers
through night back to day.
I wake up and I scream,
"Mr. Grievely, GO AWAY!!"

But there you sit, and you sit,
just beyond my clear view,
staying just close enough,
in a light cast in blue.

As I dream, I toss,
rolling and turning about.
I can sense you're STILL with me,
without any doubt.

Visions and voices,
come in and go out.
In the deafening silence
I twist and I shout.
When I'm choking on tears,
no words can come out…

In these violet-hazed nightmares
I've searched for a clue.
I'm sick to my stomach,
kind of like having the flu.

I ache and feel sore
from my hair to my shoe.
It is clear in this fog
what I need and must do.

Can I be sad and weepy?
Mr. G is this true?
I can see from your expression
that it makes you sad too.

Struggle

With a green queasy headache,
I feel like I'm bound
from your weight as you sit on me,
holding your ground;
My arms and my feet
and whole body strapped down.

Feeling trapped and confined,
I whine, tantrum and seethe.
As though shackled, constricted.
I really can't breathe.

I struggle to move
and to pry your grip free,
feeling helplessly hopeless
with this power over me.
I beg you, beast Grievely,
please just let me be!

I shouldn't be smiling
through the walls that I've built.
Brittle layers of stone
of burnt umber silt.

A numbing existence
forged in mortar of guilt.

Trapped in a dank dungeon,
I'm still dreaming I suppose.
Yearning to feel normal,
this is not what I chose!

I fake it for others
and just strike a pose.

Clenching black iron bars,
peering out in the night.
If I knew how to get past them,
don't you think that I might?

I want to feel safe,
for it to all be all right.
If only I could break out
and turn on the light.

What if my true face
mostly now stained with tears,
shows rosy bright smiles,
veiling anger and fears?

I'd be unrecognizable,
unmasked and revealed.
How can I go on without
some kind of false shield?

Exposing my terror
of not letting go.

Of dreading the happiness
I should now never show!

NO!!

I think you are mean!
My heartbeat is racing.
My invisible feet endlessly
somehow keep pacing.

Grievely, who are you?
Why and what am I chasing?

Tell me how I can take back
this life you're erasing!

Searching

On the one-hundredth morning,
living life from my bed,
you've pushed back the curtain
so I get up instead.

Gazing high over precipices,
and looking below
at a life I was used to,
but now, do not know.

The streets all look different
from this place where I stand.
Then in the midst of this madness,
something grazes my hand.

I look closely at an object
casting weight and surprise.
It glitters and sparkles.
It almost hurts my eyes!

Is this key that I'm clutching
perhaps a gift from a friend?
Grievely nods and reminds me
that this isn't the end.

What's this? Could it be
the golden key in the door?
It startles me to hear
my bare feet touch the floor.
I panic at moving towards
what is in store.

The key I turn slowly,
the door's weight creaks ajar,
then bursting wide open
to a path not so far.

There's a way to gain exit
from this barren sad land.
For just a brief moment,
I begin to understand.

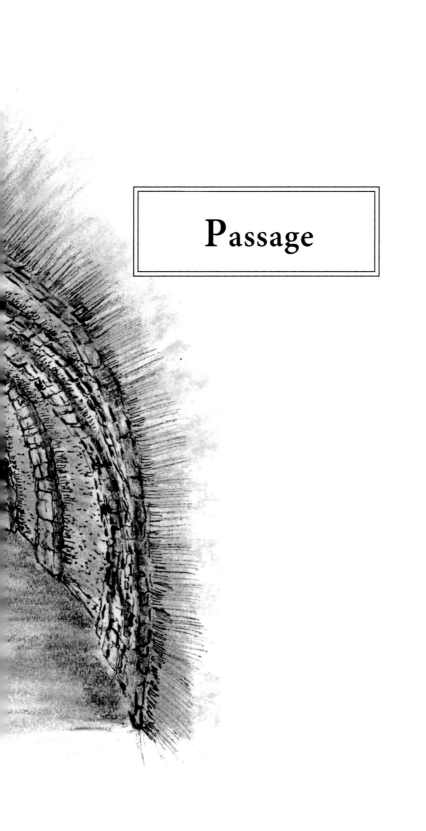

Passage

Grey mist begins lifting,
floating above and away.
I almost feel safe again.
Could this be okay?

Then gently you're behind me,
nudging me on through.
I find I'm finding courage,
and more sure of what's true.

Stepping gingerly forward
I follow your lead,
moving onward in tandem,
although not guaranteed,
I sense glimmers of happiness
gleaming in through the reeds.

Where I once was held hostage,
I'm suddenly freed.

In the distant dim horizon,
the rays increasing by day,
I'd forgotten how long
I've been hidden away.

It is you, my friend Grievely,
who has shown me the way.

And the times, when the light's on,
I can forget that you're there.
I look over or under
and you're just in that chair.

I swear it was empty,
then as clear as a star,
shining bright in the darkness,
yup, there you are!

You hand me a picture
or letter or book
you have illuminated for me,
so I may take a look at
concealed cherished memories
when love sparkled each day.

I look up and I whisper,
"Mr. Grievely, please stay!"

And there is never a time
when we're ever alone,
even though we're not able
to simply pick up the phone.

We have something far better
with which to connect.
Could you be in my heart?
Is my theory correct?
A perpetual place where
we go to reflect.

Peace

It is all coming clear!
You're a friend within reach.
I was mistaken to fear you.
You've come here to teach.

So today I bid you welcome!
Please come in and sit.
We can remain here and chat,
but just for a bit.

It is there when you
warmly sit and abide,
I feel soft yellow energy
glowing deep from inside.

From that place you remind me
there is no need to hide.
Love will always live on
where our memories reside.

Thanks to you Mr. Grievely,
I found a new me.
Yet, when we first met,
thought you were my enemy.

Thanks to you I am changed.

Renewed . . .

Rearranged.

You helped me heal
from this emotional flu.
Your patient persistence
still guides me on through.
Beyond all this sadness,
embracing changes anew.

And just to be open,
honest and clear,
I've grown attached to
the comfort in having you here.
Perpetual care is in you,
Grievely, dear.

And now looking back
over months that have passed,
it was friendship you offered.
You didn't harass.

For as you reappear
and disappear from my sight,
I will welcome your presence.
We do not have to fight!

I am certain to need you
in hard times ahead.
Sad days, or new ways,
I now need not dread.
I can confidently meet them
knowing you're there.
My friend clad in sky blue,
in that very same chair.

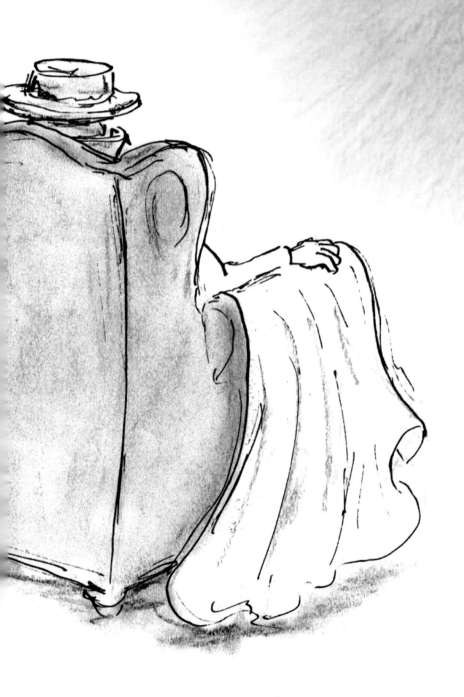

And in all sincerity,
at the risk of being impolite,
you may stay for the day,
but not well into the night.

It is a new day,
and I have the choice and the right
to enjoy the bright sunshine
and the day's brilliant light.

So stand by, Mr. G.
Please don't go astray.
And if you can't linger,
for all others I pray.
Make haste!
Greet those in darkness
who, like I, lost their way.

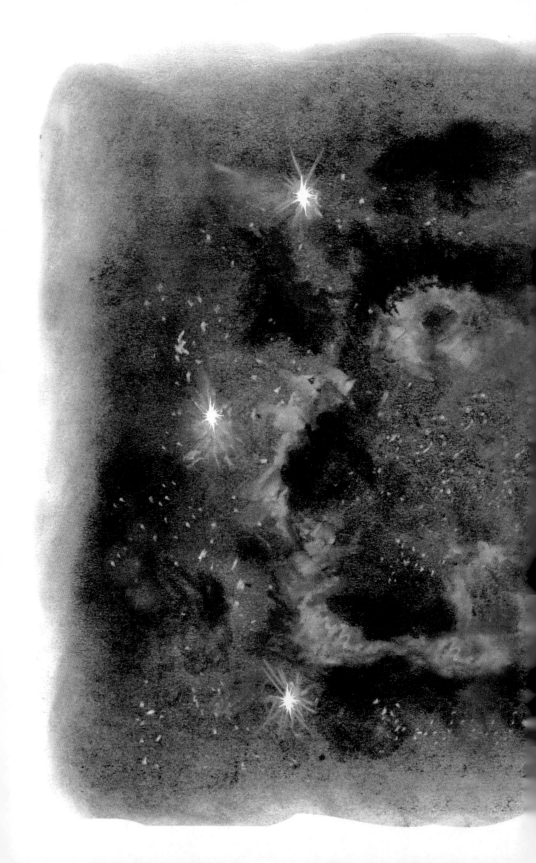

And I,
I will stand tall,
being bold if I may,
at the threshold awash
in hope's white light today.

Thanks to YOU, Mr. Grievely…

I know I'm okay.

Appreciation

This journey began one hazy late July afternoon in 2020 after sleeping deeply through my sadness. I awoke with the words in my head, "Oh woe and hello, Mr. Grievely, come in!" I was compelled to write from my bed daily, which yielded a collection of pages that became the story of "Mr. Grievely." I still cannot say from whence the words originated, and I feel I am simply a conduit through which this story was rendered. It is imperative that I offer gratitude to – and for – all those on earth and beyond, whose guidance nurtured, inspired, coaxed, critiqued and loved me through this grieving process.

Thanks to the following:
Josh Hrehovcik, (Retroroadtripper.com), friend/fellow author, for your motivation and urging to have this story illustrated and published.

Steve Hrehovcik, illustrator extraordinaire, dear friend (and Josh's Dad). My endless gratitude for countless shared transformative hours in the studio. Your hands have given brilliant light, form and texture to my words and emotions.

"Auntie Carol" Hrehovcik, for reading and re-reading text with loving enthusiastic encouragement. I am forever grateful to you for believing in this story.

David Conti, friend/brother. Your candor and insight gave form and logic to a raw and unpolished compilation of verse.

Geraldine Aikman, my beagle soul sister, creative taskmaster and muse, for your brilliance and patience! Our long creative partner/ friendship has just begun.

Elaine Dalton, from day one, and before, you had my back and held my hand.

Donna Privatera, my beloved high school English teacher, mentor and lifetime friend. I have found my voice, and with your faith in me, my wings. Thank you for the depth and breadth of your stellar influence. Grazie mio maestra e dio ti benedica amore mio.

Rebecca Mallen, Nancy Doherty Neri, and Robert Vieira, to each of you for sharing your wisdom and dedication to this story, and to Doug Bibber for your kindness, always.

God bless my league of earth angels who surround and stay me each step of the way: Renee Schneider, Becky Dore, Brenda Callagy, Marcia Mucci, Julann Cadorette, Dee Vieira, Laura Barra, Carolyn Dorsky, Teresa Kruszewski, Clare and Dennis Sullivan, Mawari Painter, Dr. Richard and Rochelle Newman, Leslie Ann Beauregard, Kate Maloney Toothaker, Gloria Swanbon, sisters Nancy Clay Castle and Trisha DiMaio Welch, and surrogate mom, Susan Clay.

To my children, Delaney and Spencer Gray. We navigate this river of tears together, heads above water; each stroke we swim brings us closer to the shore. The love legacy they left will live on through us and within our hearts always. Jackie Gamache Sausville and Deanna Gamache, my daughters from grace, thank you always for your love and support.

Finally, Ralph Gamache, the best husband ever; bound for sainthood, for sitting at the edge of the bed, listening and reading what came next. For pouring our coffee each morning, sopping up puddles of tears and pulling back the curtain; illuminating that very dark place. You carried me, and steadied my posture, making it possible for me to stand tall. You held my hand and my gaze. Your strong presence at my side and dedication has brought this mission to fruition. I love you and am grateful that God gave you to us all.

Mr. Grievely, my dear, compassionate friend, thank you for bringing me on through.

XO. Holly

Author's Reflection

There will be times in life when we share happiness and with others, sadness. It is strange and challenging how we find we have to balance life and its lessons. Sometimes we can see signs of loss coming ahead of us, giving time to understand and process. Change can also come in a split second, which can leave us very confused and lost. Especially when events create change in our lives.

It may be the loss of a very special and important person or pet. We can feel sadness after having moved to a new home, school or job, or even when something big happens in the world that we don't completely understand.

These events can all cause us anxiety and stress, making us feel out of control. Kids, adults and even animals feel these same feelings when loss and change happens. The name for this is grief.

Grieving is how we and others work through sad and scary times of change. We can have a whole bundle of different feelings that we don't understand, and we can't always know when they will come. The world can seem fine one minute and then in an unexpected instant, a wave of grief drops us to our knees, and it seems to just start all over again.

Some days we can't even describe how we are feeling and maybe can't talk about it to anyone, making our insides and head hurt. It can make us feel angry and exhausted or want to be all alone. We may even want to run away. We may wonder if we'll ever just feel normal again. The answer is, YES, we will. There is hope. We are all on a journey, and grief holds our hand each step of the way.

Feeling is remembering. Remembering is love.

Just feel.
XO, Holly

Holly Margeson Gamache is a native to New England. She is a seasoned educator with over 40 years in public education and now designs and instructs professional workforce development in higher education. She is married to her best friend Ralph, who shares and supports all of her creative endeavors. They make their home in coastal Maine with their beloved beagle, Miss Bailey, who rescued them in 2019. Holly is a mother by choice and grace to four amazing people, Spencer, Delaney, Deanna and Jacqueline.

Holly became an orphan when both her parents, Chuck and Jo Anne, took to heaven in 2019. They inspired this book, and their legacy of love continues to enrich all the lives they touched with their own. They are missed beyond measure, and their spirits continue to abide with their family members in various forms and signs.

Holly has a deep love and appreciation for Fine and Performing Arts. She is a photographer, musician and writer, and recognizes that life is a gift to be treasured each day.

Steve Hrehovcik is an award-winning artist and designer, with illustrations and graphic art appearing in numerous books, magazines, newspapers and business publications. His credits also included commissions to create paintings of portraits, homes and buildings, children's books, equestrian and pets, caricatures and cartoons, scenic views, plus reproductions of classical works of celebrated masters.

Steve is also a writer with more than 900 published articles. Other writing assignments include movie, theater and animation scripts, short stories and poetry. He has also published his book *Rebel Without a Clue – A Way-Off Broadway Memoir*, in which he describes his journey in search of a career in the theater.

He lives in Kennebunk, Maine, with his wife of 58 years, Carol.
www.kennebunkartstudio.com

Made in the USA
Middletown, DE
07 October 2023

39811132R00053